Updated 2018

TIME!
Idea-rich tips for enhanced performance and productivity

We live in an increasingly hectic and demanding world. The demands of running a business or having a career, overlap and conflict with the demands of having a life, being a spouse or parent, and enjoying the fruits of our labor. Many of us are already running as fast as we can – and we're not keeping up.

If you are like me, you may occasionally find yourself with too much on your already 'full' plate. You've said **'YES'** a few too many times without fully counting the cost or realistically estimating the time *needed* to do what you've just promised. Whew!

Over the past 20 plus years, I have had the privilege of investing my time and leveraging my **'Ideas At Work!'** with a wide range of people across the globe. I've worked with front line staff, service people, professional service providers and sales people, professional association members, leaders, business owners, entrepreneurs, executives, and managers. I hear leaders and their teams telling me, *"…life is good; but, out of control, over-committed, and with a blurring lack of focus on the important things and people in their lives."*

TIME! was designed for those who are **"Running TOO FAST!"** (available from www.SuccessPublications.ca) It is written by someone who has learned the value of leveraging his investment of **'TIME!'** for greater success and productivity. You can too!

Bob 'Idea Man' Hooey

Table of contents

Table of contents 3

Chapter 1: TIME! *Idea-rich tips for enhanced performance and productivity* 4

Chapter 2: How much is your time *really* worth? 7

Chapter 3: From 'KAI-ZEN' to 'I CAN!' 9

Improvement = Consistent commitment to good change 9

Chapter 4: Identifying and eliminating your time wasters 17

Chapter 5: Cherish Today! 19

Chapter 6: P*R*I*O*R*I*T*I*E*S 20

Chapter 7: Four P's of Personal Performance 23

Chapter 8: Converting Filler Time to Foundation Time 25

Chapter 9: Bob's Time Tricks 29

Chapter 10: Secrets of a procrastinator - It's about time, 'YOUR' time! 30

Copyright and license notes 32

Acknowledgements, credits, and disclaimers 33

Bob's B.E.S.T. publications 35

What they say about Bob 'Idea Man' Hooey 37

Chapter 1: TIME!
Idea-rich tips for enhanced performance and productivity

Finish your race and still have a life! If you are like me, you may occasionally find yourself with too much on your already **'full'** plate. You've said **'YES'** a few too many times, without counting the cost, or estimating the time *needed* to do what you've just promised. As a prolific writer and globe-trotting speaker I am constantly tempted to take on 'just one more client', 'just one more engagement', or 'just one more writing project.' In doing so, I often find myself staying up late to meet commitments and/or rushing from airport to venue.

Sound familiar? Welcome to the **overcommitted club!** If this is just a momentary or temporary overload, you can dig in and work your way through it; or wait until you can get a handle on the commitments you've made. Then, you can relax, and get back to a more **normal schedule.**

But, if this is your **'life', then this little book is for you!** I'd suggest a long pause… to reflect and refocus; may be **d-e-s-p-e-r-a-t-e-l-y** in order.

Take hope – take action! You can make the necessary changes to free up your time for the important people and priorities in your life. It can be done, and you can do it! With the death of both my parents in 1999, I had a chance to review and refocus my life and my career. I also had time to finish a few writing projects while caring for my mom until she too passed away. When Irene and I got married 10 years ago, my priorities and time commitments changed, for the better.

First, let's clear up the misnomer of **'time management.'** Time cannot really be managed. We can manage others and ourselves in relation to time, but we cannot manage time itself.

It will keep ticking along, slipping through our fingers like the *sands in an hourglass*, even when we wish it wouldn't.
We can control how and where we spend or invest our time.

Life or SELF-management, based on value-based judgements, is what is meant when we use the words 'time management.' The time management techniques briefly shared here can easily save you an hour or more each day. The real question is... **"What will you do with those extra hours?"** Where will you strategically invest them?

"No doubt overcommitted people find help in better time management techniques, but many of them will use their newfound skills to pack more obligations into their lives, rather than step back from their madcap pace."
Howard Macy

Take a moment...

Decide right NOW where the extra time you free up will be invested. Will your family reap the long-term benefits of better management of your time? Will you spend more effective time building your self-esteem by preparing yourself to meet the challenges of our quickly changing world? Will you choose to invest this recaptured time in helping others? Will you invest time doing something fun?

**It's your time!
Why not choose to invest it more wisely?**

Bob 'Idea Man' Hooey

Japanese 23rd Psalm

When stress overwhelms you, the Japanese version of the 23rd Psalm can be very helpful...

The Lord is my Pacesetter, I shall not rush.
He makes me stop for quiet intervals;
He provides me with pictures of stillness,
Which restores my serenity.
He leads me in the way of efficiency through
calmness of mind, His guidance is peace.
Even though I have a great many things to
accomplish each day, I will not fret,
for His presence is with me.
His timelessness, His importance,
will keep me in balance.
He prepares refreshment and renewal in
the midst of any activity by anointing me
with the oil of his tranquility.
My cup of joyous energy overflows.
Surely harmony and effectiveness
shall be the fruit of my hours, and I
shall walk in the pace of the Lord,
and dwell in
His house forever.

Author Unknown

Chapter 2: How much is your time *'really'* worth?

Have you ever taken a moment to think about what your time is *really* worth? Have you ever calculated your earning capacity on an hourly or on a quarterly (15 min) basis? This can be a great exercise in determining your worth, relative value, and earning contribution. It can also tell you how much 'each' hour you allow to be wasted is really costing you.

Let's figure it out together.

Let's take a typical example; assuming 52, 5-day weeks in a year. We will deduct 2, 5-day weeks for normal vacation time. This leaves us 250 days. Then, deduct the holidays.

In Canada, we have 10-12 holidays per year, so let's take 10. This will leave us with only 240 work days in which to earn our salary or money.

Assuming an average 8-hour workday this gives us **1920 'potential' work hours in a year.**

On the surface, we'd simply take our Gross Pay and divide by the hours, e.g. $50,000/year would give us an average hourly rate of $26.04 per hour. So, in this instance each 15-minute block of recaptured or **wasted time would be costing you $6.51.**

Let's take this a bit further, shall we? In all honesty, would you say that you are able to get a **'full'** 8 productive hours in each 8-hour day? No? Me either! If you are in sales how much of your time is spent selling or servicing your clients? If you are in leadership, how much of your time is spent working with your team?

My contention, based on feedback from thousands of our North American audience members, is the 'true productivity number' is somewhere closer **to 60% effectiveness on any given day.** Perhaps, in some instances, that is optimistic. Let's go with that for this exercise. If that is true, then we really have only 1152 work hours in which to make our money.

In the previous example, each hour would *now* be worth $43.40 and each 15-minute block wasted would cost us $10.85.

Here are some rough comparisons for different dollar earning levels

Annual Earnings	Hourly rate	60% Effective rate	15 min. block
50,000/year	$26.04	$43.40	$10.85
100,000/year	$52.08	$86.80	$21.70
200,000/year	$104.16	$173.60	$43.40

Very interesting figures, aren't they? If you are aware of what your time is 'really' worth it will help you keep an eye on the time wasters that creep into your life. Not that I put a monetary price on everything in my life; but it is good to know what my 'investment' is **worth**.

If you are aware of how you 'presently' use time, you will be better equipped to make the changes to make better use of it in the future.

After my dad died in 1999, I spent quite a lot of time with my mom before she passed away a short 6 months later. It was probably the best return for my investment I've ever made - priceless!

I'd do it again, in a heartbeat, if I could. I would give anything to spend just a little bit of time with either of them.

Chapter 3: From 'KAI-ZEN' to 'I CAN!'
Improvement = Consistent commitment to good change

Kai = *change*   **Zen** = *good*
When they are used together = *improvement*

Kai-zen came to popularity in North America during the mid-1980's, after becoming an integral part of the Japanese management theory. Western management consultants used it to embrace a wide-range of management practices, which were regarded as primarily Japanese. These practices were thought to be the secrets of the strength of Japanese companies in the areas of continual improvement rather than innovation.

According to this theory, the strength of Japanese organizations lay in their attention to 'process' rather than simply results. They concentrated the team efforts to continually improve imperfections at each stage of the process. According to them, over the long-term, the result was more reliable, of better quality, more advanced and attractive to clients, and less expensive than Western Management practices.

Its roots however are from an American influence following the 2nd World War. **General Douglas MacArthur** approached several leading US experts to visit Japan to advise them on how to proceed with rebuilding their country and their economy. One such expert was **Dr. Edwards Deming (1900-1993).**

He initially came to Japan to conduct a census but noticed the newly emerging industries were having difficulty. He had been involved in reducing waste in US War manufacturing and drew on that experience to offer his advice. By the 1950's, he was a regular visitor, offering advice to Japanese manufacturers that were having challenges in terms of raw materials, components, and investment; additionally, suffering from low morale in the nation and workforce. By the 1970's, many of Japan's leading organizations had embraced Dr. Deming's key points for management. Most are as valid today as a half-century ago.

Here are some that relate specifically to the concept called Kai-zen.

An improved philosophy to effectively deal with change and client needs.
Constant pursuit of purpose required for improvement of products and services.
Improving 'every' process for planning, production, and service.
Instituting or embedding on-going, on the job training for all staff using a variety of methods and ideas.
Instituting and supporting leadership that is aimed and focused on helping people do a better job. *(Isn't that the true purpose of 21st Century leadership and management?)*
Breaking down the barriers and boundaries that exist within departments and people. *(GE's CEO, Jack Welsh took this one on personally in his style of management.)*
Encouraging education for the self-improvement of every member of the organization.
Top management is committed to improve *'all'* these points, specifically quality and leadership.

Adapting the Kai-zen attitude to our western way of doing business requires a **'major change in corporate culture'** – creating a corporate culture that:
Admits openly and honestly there are problems and challenges.
Encourages a positive, collaborative, consultative attitude to solving or overcoming them.
Actively 'devolves' responsibility to the most appropriate or effective level. The person who is in the best position to deal with the challenge or problem needs to have the time, the tools, and the authority to do so.
Promotes continuous skills-based training and development of attitudes.

Traditionally, the Japanese approach embedded Kai-zen in its hierarchical structure, although it gives substantially more responsibilities within certain fixed boundaries.

The key features of this management approach and focus are:

Attention to process, rather than results: Analyze every part of the process down to the smallest detail, with a view to improving them. Looks at how employee's actions, equipment, and materials can be improved.

Cross-functional management: Management team has an expanded focus to help improve the process and the skills of the people outside the typical western turf wars.

Use of quality circles; and other tools to support their commitment to continuous improvement.

A range of tools have been developed, along the KAI-ZEN line, to assist companies to make tangible improvements:

Quality Control Circles: groups of people whose primary focus and purpose is to continually improve quality.

Process-oriented management: more attention focused on the 'how' (the process) rather than the 'what' (the task).

Visible management: top executives are being seen, 'walking the job' (management by walking around) and being available to 'see' and consult on each stage of the process.

Cross-functional management: working across functional divides and typical barriers or boundaries, to provide more unity, sense of team, and a wider vision that engages and involves everyone.

Just-in-time management: control of stock and other materials and components to avoid unnecessary expenditures.

PDCA: a process of **P**lan, **D**o, **C**heck, **A**ct to assist in solving challenges.

Statistical process control: enable each machine operator or member of a team to control and measure quality at each stage of the process.

In the Japanese approach to Kai-zen, all these tools are used in a holistic manner. Contrast this to the current western approach where some of these tools are individually introduced as the 'answer' to every problem or challenge, without consideration of the context within which they were designed to work effectively.

Some perceived benefits of this Kai-zen type of approach:

Can lead to a reduction of 'wasted' time and resources
Can increase productivity
Relatively easy to introduce – requires no major capital investment
Can lower the break-even point
Enables organizations to react quickly to market changes
Appropriate for fast and slow economies as well as growing or mature markets

However, we face some **challenges of introducing Kai-zen** into the western management mind-set.

It can be difficult to achieve Kai-zen in practice, as it requires a complete or major change in attitude and culture. It needs the energy and commitment of all employees as well as leaders. It also requires a substantive investment of time by leaders and their respective teams.

It can be difficult to maintain enthusiasm for several reasons: some see Kai-zen as a threat to their jobs; poor ideas tend to be put forward along with good ideas, which can at times be de-motivating; by implication, there is never complete satisfaction.

Continuous improvement is not sufficient or a stand-alone approach in itself. Major innovation is still needed. There is a danger of becoming 'evolutionary' in focus to the exclusion of being 'revolutionary' or innovation sensitive.

In this turbulent, global economy, organizations need to look at all methods, tools, techniques, and training processes that might help in this quest for growth. Kai-zen's step-by-step approach is in direct contrast to the great leaps forward many organizations experience via the innovation avenue.

It is almost as though we need to develop a 'bi-focal' approach and viewpoint, which is one that encompasses steady, continuous improvement of current processes, products, and services; while looking for and encouraging creativity and innovation in moving the organization to the next level. (*I do this in the development of my various training programs and publications.*)

Kai-zen should free up time for senior managers to think about the long-term future of the organization, look for new opportunities, and move to a concentration on 'strategic' issues. Kai-zen can support improvement of 'existing' activities; but it will not provide the impetus for the innovation process, which often provides our great leaps forward. A balanced approach is called for here.

It is the role of 'strategic' leadership to take responsibility for the implementation of an effective corporate mission (purpose or soul), reward, and the organizational structure.

It is the responsibility of 'tactical and strategic' managers to model and practice sound leadership, to promote good teamwork, and to work to ensure everyone understands their roles and the process itself.

It is the responsibility of 'everyone' in the organization (from front-line to senior management), to measure themselves and their teams; to identify in quantifiable, measurable terms, areas for improvement; and to generate ideas to change practice and procedures. Then, continue measurement to ensure this improvement has been achieved, recorded, and celebrated. Each time it is measured, it can be analyzed, and a new standard achieved or set and measured. This becomes the cycle of continual improvement. (I CAN!)

Here is a typical or suggested 'cycle' or process:
generate ideas
evaluate ideas
decide on action
plan implementation
design measurement system
take action
set new standard
measure
analyze
define problem/desired state
identify areas for improvement
generate ideas

Everyone on your team needs to be 'totally' committed to this cycle of continuous improvement. Each team member must be given the knowledge, skills, and tools to be able to participate fully and enthusiastically. They need to participate, not only within their own respective teams; but also, across the organization, as a part of a cross-functional team.

For this to become a reality, work must be undertaken to reinforce or build the confidence within your staff to take on greater responsibility or make decisions for themselves.

This is an underlying foundation to the work we did in writing and creating *'The Brick Way – It's about ALL of us'* for a major Canadian Retailer.

We wanted to send and support the message of each member of their 7000-member team taking additional responsibilities and personal leadership over their respective roles. We wanted to instill a new culture and work to create a *'Company of Leaders'*.

This reinforcement is crucial to Kai-Zen's success. In addition to specific skills training and use of tools and knowledge, it is important for us to work on the 'climate for change'; to ensure it is embedded in our corporate culture.

The core values within a Kai-zen based approach to which each of us can aspire are:

Trust and respect for every member of the team across the organization, not just his or her own team. (Not just their department, their own specialization, expertise, or level.) Each individual on a team should be able to openly admit any mistakes or failings they've made or exist in their role and work on doing a better job the next time. Responsibility is an individual commitment. Progress is impossible without the ability to admit, learn from, and move forward from mistakes.

Quite a few years back, I listened to *'A Power Talk'* CD from **Tony Robbins**, in which he shared his concept of CANI (Constant and Never-ending Improvement) for use in our day-to-day lives and roles as leaders. He was quite passionate about his commitment to this concept and for its implementation in our daily lives. He advocated a commitment to constant and never-ending improvement.

I'd like to take a 'robbins-esque' approach, and challenge each of you to take a moment to digest what we've discussed about this transplanted US – filtered through Japan approach to management, as a part of your leadership role.
I reworded it to a more positive focused **'I CAN'** acronym.
Improvement is continual and never ending.

If you and your team are going to be successful in taking your organization to the next level of growth, each of you will need to get a firm foundation and focus on the process of Kai-zen style continual improvement.

This is in addition to your personal leadership in applied innovation or **Ideas At Work!** - as they apply to your changing roles and the teams you seek to lead.

My challenge for each of you: Develop an 'I CAN!' approach and attitude to your leadership and team management, and to equip and inspire those you would seek to lead. 'Improvement is continual and never ending' and it starts with me!'

You can use this 'I CAN' Kai-Zen based focus in your quest to free up time that you choose to reinvest in the lives and skills of those you lead.

Enjoy the journey! In the 'Kai-zen' or 'I CAN!' world, the journey is the goal and provides the sense of achievement and satisfaction. It really works for top performing leaders and their teams as they remain committed to continual improvement in how they leverage their time and enhance their productivity.

"What we need to do is learn to work in the system; by which I mean that everybody, every team, every platform, every division, every component is there not for individual competitive profit or recognition, but for contribution to the system as a whole on a win-win basis."
W. Edwards Deming

Chapter 4: Identifying and eliminating your time wasters

Over the years, we've asked our audiences about their time challenges, and been able to identify the **25 most common, biggest time wasters.**

"If time and priority management is not an 'integral', daily part of what you '*are*' doing; all the technology/tools, as well as these idea-rich strategies and time management success systems will be wasted."

Here they are! Our audiences across North America have helped us come up with some novel approaches to help combat them.

Telephone interruptions
Failure to plan
Attempting TOO much
Drop-in Visitors
Socializing (can now include social media) and daydreaming
Ineffective or non-existent delegation
Travel (commuting)
Lack of self-discipline
Inability to say NO!
Procrastination or making 'busy' work
Family concerns
Paper work - *where is the paperless office they promised us?*
Leaving tasks unfinished
Not enough staff or personnel
Meetings *(unnecessary or unproductive)*
Confused responsibility - *I thought you were going to do that?*
Poor verbal and written communication skills
Inadequate controls, feedback, or progress reports

Inaccurate information
Personal and corporate disorganization
Faxes and email *(great if targeted and used appropriately)*
Management by CRISIS!
Cell phones and pagers *(they can be great if used properly)*
Television
Surfing the Internet and social media
(ok...I get caught up in it too!) www.ideaman.net

You may have some of your own time wasters, not on this list. Take a moment to honestly appraise your life and activities.

Go through this list. Check off the time wasters you recognize, *(and remember the people who employ them against you)*, that are draining your schedule and energy. Once you've identified the major ones, decide to work on each one until you've mastered it.

Successful life and time management is a journey not a destination. As in any journey, the starting point is just as important as the destination. Start where you are with a solid focus of where you want to go. Then go for it!

One tip: Don't try to deal with them all at once. Select a few, and work on them, until you've beaten them. Then confidently tackle the next ones on your list. It may take some time, but... if you focus your energies. **You can take control!**

"There are always two choices, two paths to take. One is easy and that is its only reward."
Unknown

Chapter 5: Cherish Today!

"Yesterday is but a dream, tomorrow a vision of hope. Look to this day, for it is life. I cannot change yesterday. I can only make the most of today and look with hope toward tomorrow!" Anonymous

Review the list of time wasters. Pick your top five and put them on this list. Take a few minutes and jot down what you think is the real cause (be brutally honest now) and discuss possible solutions with your friends and colleagues. Then set a start time and date when you **'WILL' put your best choice, strategy, or solution into practice.**

As you discuss some of these time wasters, new ideas may pop into your mind. Write them down and share them with your friends. **Brainstorm real solutions to real problems... then commit immediately to put those ideas into action!**

Being able to find something quickly, when you need it, frees up your time for more creative and productive endeavors.

Chapter 6: P*R*I*O*R*I*T*I*E*S

"A hundred years from now it will not matter what size my back account was, the sort of house I lived in, or the kind of car I drove...but the world may be different because I was important in the life of a child." Anonymous

One helpful suggestion in your life and time management might be in being crystal clear on your priorities in life and business. Remaining focused on the priorities in your personal and family life makes it easier to balance and blend them with the demands of your business, community, and career priorities. Far too many of us have personally paid the price for being unbalanced in our priorities and have lost partners and families. These needless personal tragedies could have been avoided, **if we'd only invested the time!**

Someone challenged me, that to be truly effective in my life, I should begin to *"schedule my priorities instead of just prioritizing my schedule."* This subtle, strategic change has made a major difference in results and the accompanied lifestyle benefits.

Knowing what your priorities are and scheduling specific time each week to work on them brings freedom. **It helps you say "NO!" to demands that don't fall in line or would distract you from seeing your priorities fulfilled.** You are better informed and able to evaluate decisions, time investments, resource allotments, and specific goals. You can become more productive when you are working on the important projects in your career. You become more fulfilled when you spend time with the more important people in your life.

I'd suggest spending a few moments on a regular basis revisit and revise your priorities.

PLAN monthly, SCHEDULE weekly, and LIVE daily!

Take a moment and make a note to yourself about these various areas and your priorities. Spend time later to refine and focus your thoughts. Keep your written priorities clear, concise, and focused.

Update them regularly. Ask yourself... what is the one most important activity I can do this week or today to help me reach my goals in this specific area?

I've used the following five to help me keep focused.

FAMILY:

SELF-IMPROVEMENT:

CAREER:

COMMUNITY:

SPIRITUAL/SPORTS/HOBBIES:

In my case, I routinely schedule my **focused five** activities, as outlined here. I take a careful look at my goals and areas of concern and try to schedule the five most important activities first. Then, I schedule the remainder of my activities. This has made a tremendous difference in my productivity and life!

You might want to add a couple more areas or redefine them to help make it more focused for you. I might suggest adding:

WORK/BUSINESS: (separate from career)

PERSONAL: (separate from family and others)

If you've taken the time to fill out this section, I'd like to commend you. Did you realize that you have now done what 95% of your fellow North Americans never have? Most North Americans have never taken even a few minutes to look at their lives and give some serious thought to their goals and values. **And they wonder why their lives have been less than productive and fulfilling.**

This time of reflection and refocus can be a pivotal point in gaining effective control of your time and life. Please take the time to pause and ponder your priorities. It is worth it!

Harness the power of your schedule

Successful people create routines and schedules that allow them to focus their energies on the most important activities needed. They know the value of applied habit and routine as proven by champions in every field. They work to streamline their schedules and minimize those activities that distract them. They plan for success and build strong success habits.

Prioritize one item per day. Focus on your highest value or one of your 'vital few' activities that moves you forward.

Use a 'Focused Five' approach as you plan your work week.

Schedule email and return phone calls. Group them.

No meetings unless they are decisive. Guard your time!

Set a daily routine. Build success habits that allow you to win.

Manage the mornings. Do your vital few activities first thing.

Do something easy first – to kick start your day. Success to start.

Never schedule more than 50% of your day. Life happens amid our schedule, so plan for it.

Build in flex time to allow for 'interruptions'. Schedule more time than you think something will take. I suggest 125%, as a rule.

Chapter 7: Four P's of Personal Performance

Our days will be more effectively used, when we plan or block out our time, based on what I call the **4 P's of Personal Performance.** And in brief, here they are:

PEOPLE/PAY DAYS: Our success in life and business is often directly related to our ability to relate and work with people. In business, our success is very dependent on maintaining good working relationships with our co-workers, our employees, our employers, our suppliers, our competition, and most importantly our clients or customers.

Simply put, **a people/pay day** is one where the **major** focus is on finding, building, and maintaining the relationships that are important in your life and business. Spending time nurturing and augmenting these relationships can work miracles in team building, customer loyalty, and business longevity.

POWER/PAPERWORK DAY: There are days when the deadlines, the commitments, and the process of running our business and career needs to be our **major** focus. And rightly so! The work needs to be done, the business must be managed, and the bills and orders must be processed. **Power/Paperwork days** are the days in which **we set aside blocks of un-interrupted time** to focus on specific projects or obligations and work through to make sure they are completed properly and on schedule.

Days - when the work must be about the work – really do WORK!

PAUSE/PLAY DAY: There are days when we need to regenerate, to relax, to take a break from our labour, to enjoy our families, and sometimes to daydream or even goof-off. Days, in which we have fun, not focused on building a business, or in pursuit of training that will advance our careers.

Maybe we take a **'fun'** course in something unrelated to what we do - just for the **joy of learning.** Maybe we take part of an afternoon off and sit quietly on a swing, watching the clouds as they slowly meander across the sky.

Pause/Play days allow us to reflect and refocus our energies, priorities and resources; and **make life worthwhile!** They are most effective in helping us regain control and in balancing our power and people days to maximize our effectiveness. They are critical components to a successful life!

PLANNING/PREP DAY: These are days allocated, monthly or quarterly, to plan and work 'on' the business, not 'in' the business; days when the focus is on strategic planning, analysis, and other functions of a long-range perspective.

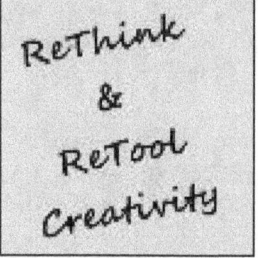

We cover this area in more detail in **Running TOO Fast!** available from **www.SuccessPublications.ca**

People spend and excessive amount of time conjugating three verbs: **To Want, To Have, To Do.** *We had forgotten that* **"To Be"** *is the source and fount of life.*
Unknown

TIME OFF - the ultimate perk!

Every year the Gallup, Harris, and Roper Polls conduct surveys to see what North Americans value highest. Since 1988 these polls have indicated North Americans wanted more time off to be with their families and do other activities instead of work. This was a major shift from the previous years. Sure, has been for me!

How does this goal rank in your life?

How will you schedule more time off this year?

Chapter 8: Converting Filler Time to Foundation Time

One of the secrets to regaining control of your time and life is in the strategic conversion of 'filler' or wasted time into 'foundation' or constructive time. Recapturing those seemingly ***'insignificant'*** slices of time (5 to 15-minute chunks) and converting them to constructive use will make a major difference in your life, career advancement, and long-term business or leadership success.

What I'd like to suggest here are a few ideas that might help you do just that - capture those 'insignificant' minutes and convert them to useful time.

Useful time, that builds a foundation for success under your dreams and goals.

Useful time, that leads you productively in the direction you've laid out for your future.

Useful time, that previously was wasted or thrown away.

Feel free to add your own suggestions. If you have some new or unique ideas, I'd love to hear them and will include them in subsequent printings of this work. (email bhooey@mcsnet.ca)

At home...
Bunch or group your errands and activities.
Spend 5-10 minutes each day planning your schedule and activities.
Trade off with neighbours or friends and share common chores - i.e., kids to school.
Use your time in the shower as planning time to mentally go over your daily schedule.

Coordinate and lay out your business clothing before you go to bed.

Coordinate your business clothing to include suits, shirts, ties, accessories, etc. Or, blouses, skirts, jackets, etc.

Never make more than one trip, if possible. Don't backtrack!

Use a voice mail system on your phone. Some systems can assign voice mailboxes for each family member. With the advent of cell phones, this may not be as valid.

Open your mail over a recycling bin.

Limit your TV time and watch what brings value to you.

Read something that enriches your life, inspires your soul, or adds value to your career or business.

Limit your internet time checking social media or playing on line games. This has evolved into a major black 'time sucking' hole for many people in our audiences.

Multi-task to combine activities that would normally demand down time or waiting time, for example, cooking and laundry or menu planning.

Agree on a special family time to discuss and plan family activities.

At work…

Spend 5-10 minutes each day reviewing the current day and planning activities and goals for the next day. Revise your schedule based on 4 P's of Personal Performance principles. (People/Pay days; Power/Paperwork day; Pause/Play day; and Planning/Prep day.)

Keep a folder with required reading close at hand for those 'on-hold' fun times.

Keep a career enhancement book (print, eBook, or reader format) close at hand for creative reading breaks.

Open your business mail over your wastebasket.

Batch your phone calls for specific times each day.

Where feasible, return phone calls at specific times each day.
Where feasible, return your emails at specific times each day.
Minimize your time on Facebook, LinkedIn, and YouTube while at work, or working on a time sensitive project.
Unless you are doing research, keep your surfing to a minimum.
Plan what you are going to say before you make a call and have the relevant information or files available for quick reference.
Multi-task to do more than one job, alternating back and forth between activities instead of just waiting for something to warm up, print, or load.
Trade off with co-workers to create some 'un-interrupted' planning and creative time.

While waiting...
Carry a book (e-reader) or something to read with you.
Use your Cell phone to retrieve and return messages.
Have a mini-recorder to dictate letters or brainstorm ideas.
This might be a good time to check and return emails.
This might also be a great time to tweet, check your Facebook, or other social media accounts.

While commuting...
Turn your car into a mobile university - listen to audiotapes, MP3s, or CDs enroute.
If using public systems - use a personal MP3 or CD player and ear phones.
If you are on the phone, make sure you are using a hands-free device. Many areas are now fining distracted drivers.
Spend the time revising your schedule and revisiting your priorities and goals.

While traveling...
Pre-select your seat whenever possible. Most airlines will allow you to do this in advance of coming to airport.

Print your boarding pass ahead of time or download to your Smart Phone. Pack light to save time checking in and waiting at the luggage carousel.

Carry selected reading to review enroute. I now carry a Kobo loaded with a mix of business and fiction books.

Take along postcards to send notes and thank yous to selected friends, clients, suppliers, and other important people in your life.

Take time to review and plan your week in relation to 4 P's of Personal Performance.

Take the time to specifically plan and revise your planning tool. Review magazines and articles that apply to your field of study.

I realize the above are not the 'end all - be all' of how to recapture your time. The exercise here was to show you a few examples of areas where you could reclaim a few minutes here and there to free up time for better or more productive use. As you become more focused on recapturing and reclaiming your time, you'll become aware of a multitude of ideas and activities that you can use to convert your filler time into foundation time.

Don't despise those *'insignificant'* minutes. Just like the 'secret' of compound interest, those minutes if captured and reinvested in your career or future will pay fabulous dividends.

If you come up with some unique or creative ideas would you, please email me and share them? If included in subsequent versions of this work, we will credit you and send you a copy of the updated version. bhooey@mcsnet.ca

"Carpo Momento" - seize the moment!

Chapter 9: Bob's Time Tricks

1. Use lists (Specific kinds)

Projects list – big picture, strategic-outcomes
Next Actions – next steps on active projects
Waiting for – items depending on others
STOP DOING lists – learn to say 'NO!'
Calendar – tracks time specific appointments/actions
Maybe/someday list – discretionary tasks (fillers)

2. In-box strategy

Get to the bottom of it daily!
One item at a time!
Never put something back in!

3. Two-minute rule

Any action item that takes less than 2 minutes
DO IT NOW!

4. Weekly rule

Part of the **Plan monthly; Schedule weekly, Live daily** process of effective self-management in relation to how you allocate your time.

Bonus reminder or 'nudge'

How about putting items by the door that you need to take with you in the morning? Works when going home as well.

Chapter 10: Secrets of a procrastinator - It's about time, 'YOUR' time!

"Next time, I'm not going to leave it until the last minute." Ever said that?

I have and all too often - in the past! Ever notice how that happens? We start off with all sorts of good intentions and somehow, we end up rushing, under pressure, stressed to complete a task that would have been a breeze, if ONLY, we had done it earlier.

"At times," said **Emerson**, *"the whole world seems to be in a conspiracy to importune you - with emphatic trifles."*

The secret, amid our often hectic, fast paced, activity driven life is in our discerning and sidestepping those trivial demands; to remain focused and active on the important ones vs. the urgent ones.

"TODAY, is an important day!" according to **Zig Ziglar**, *"No matter how you spend it, you will have traded a day of your life for it!"* Based on an improved age span of 85 years, we have ONLY 31,046 days to LIVE! Roughly 745,000 hours in which to live out our dreams, accomplish our life goals, and make an impact on our world and those with whom we share it.

"Do you love life? Then do not squander time," said **Benjamin Franklin**; *"for TIME is the stuff that life is made of."*

As a recovering PROCRASTINATOR, I offer these **four suggestions** to help control and conquer time, and truly live your life.

DEVOTE time to your goals. Make sure you know where it is you really want to go, what you really want to accomplish, and what *impact* statement you want your life to make. Spend time analyzing, refining, and prioritizing. As little as 15 minutes a day could impact a lifetime. Make sure these goals are realistic and compatible with your life message. Then, get on with them. DO IT NOW!

LEARN TO LEVERAGE your time by networking with others, by delegating or sharing tasks, by asking colleagues for help, and by seeking their energy, information, and resource sharing.

CREATE TIME like **Thomas Edison** who set aside a 'portion' of each day for the creative processes. Use this designated *creative time* to brainstorm, mind map goals and objectives, and to reflect on the organization, timing, and implementation of your goals. Use this creative time to dream BIG and leverage visualization techniques to allow yourself to establish your own pace and direction.

DON'T WASTE YOUR TIME. How many of us, could find at least 15-20 minutes a day that we now squander? According to Goethe, *"One always has enough time, provided one spends it well" What difference would that make?*

Your life and time management lie within your hands. It is within your power to choose to invest it well for your benefit and the benefit of those you love. Or, you can choose to let others rob you of your life's blood or squander it on useless pursuits. It is your choice - and it's about time!

But, what if you find yourself overwhelmed with commitments? How do I get out from under them you may ask? Hopefully you've garnered some ideas in this little book!

Copyright and license notes

'TIME! (Updated 3rd edition)
Idea-rich tips for enhanced performance and productivity

Bob 'Idea Man' Hooey, Accredited Speaker, 2011 Spirit of CAPS recipient. Prolific author of 30 plus business, leadership, and career success publications

© Copyright 1999-2018 Bob 'Idea Man' Hooey

All rights reserved worldwide *No part of this publication may be retained, copied, sold, rented or loaned, transmitted, reproduced, broadcast, performed or distributed in any such medium, or by any means, nor stored in any computer or distributed over any network without permission in writing from the publisher and/or author. Care has been taken to trace ownership of copyright material contained in this volume. Graphics are royalty free or under license. The publisher will gladly receive information that will allow him to rectify any reference or credit line in subsequent editions. Segments of this publication were originally published as articles and/or parts of other books and program materials and are included here by permission of the publishers and authors.* Unattributed quotations are by Bob 'Idea Man' Hooey.

Cover design: **Wendy** (craftarc)
Photos of Bob: **Dov Friedman**, www.photographybyDov.com
Bonnie-Jean McAllister, www.elantraphotography.com
Editorial, layout and design: **Irene Gaudet,** Vitrak Creative Services, vitrakcreative.com

ISBN 13: 978-1986768450   ISBN 10: 1986768457

Printed in the United States 10 9 8 7 6 5 4 3 2 1
Success Publications – a division of Creativity Corner Inc.
Box 10, Egremont, AB T0A 0Z0
www.successpublications.ca
Creative office: 1-780-736-0009

Acknowledgements, credits, and disclaimers

As with each of my books, a very special dedication of this piece of myself, to the two people who meant the most to me, my folks **Ron and Marge Hooey**. Sadly, both my parents left this earthly realm in 1999. I still miss our time together and your encouragement and love. I was blessed with the two of you in my life. I've added **George and Lillian Sidor** (Irene's folks) to this gratitude list.

To my inspiring wife and professional proof reader and publications coach, **Irene Gaudet**, who loves, encourages, and supports me in my quest to continue sharing my **Ideas At Work!** across the world. Thank you seems so inadequate for your timely work in helping make my writing and my client service better! I love the time we spend together!

To my colleagues and friends in the National Speakers Association (NSA), the Canadian Association of Professional Speakers (CAPS), and the Global Speakers Federation (GSF) who continually challenge me to strive for success and increased excellence.

To my great audiences, leaders, students, coaching clients, and readers across the globe who share their experiences and enjoyment of my work. Your positive and supportive feedback encourages me to keep working on additional programs and success publications like this updated version. My experience with you creates the foundation for additional real-life experiences I can take from the stage to the page, the classroom to the boardroom.

My thanks to a select few friends for your ongoing support and 'constructive' abuse. You know who you are. ☺

Disclaimer

We have not attempted to cite all the authorities and sources consulted in the preparation of this book. To do so would require much more space than is available. The list would include departments of various governments, libraries, industrial institutions, periodicals, and many individuals. Inspiration was drawn from many sources, including other books by the author; in this updated creation of "TIME!'

This book is written and designed to provide information on more effective use of your time, as a life and leadership enhancement guide. It is sold with the 'explicit' understanding that the publisher and/or the author are not engaged in rendering legal, accounting, or other Professional services. If legal or other expert assistance is required, the services of a competent Professional in your geographic area should be sought.

It is not the purpose of this book to reprint all the information that is otherwise available. Its primary purpose is to complement, amplify, and supplement other books and reference materials already available. You are encouraged to search out and study all the available material, learn as much as possible, and tailor the information to your individual needs. This will help to enhance your success in being a more effective sales person, leader or professional.

Every effort has been made to make this book as complete and as accurate as possible within the scope of its focus. However, there may be mistakes, both typographical and in content or attribution. Graphics are royalty free or under license. Care has been taken to trace ownership of copyright material contained in this volume. The publisher will gladly receive information that will allow him to rectify any reference or credit line in subsequent editions. This book should be used only as a general guide and not as the ultimate source of information. Furthermore, this book contains information that is current only up to the date of publication.

The purpose of 'TIME!' is to educate and entertain; perhaps to inform and to inspire. It is certainly to challenge its readers to learn and apply its secrets and tips, to challenge them to enhance their skills and leverage their time to create more Productive outcomes. The author and publisher shall have neither liability nor responsibility to any person or entity with respect to any loss or damage caused, or alleged to have been caused, directly or indirectly, by the information contained in this book.

Bob's B.E.S.T. publications

Bob is a prolific author who has been capturing and sharing his wisdom and experience in print and electronic formats for the past fifteen plus years. In addition to the following publications, several of them best sellers, he has written for consumer, corporate, trade, professional associations, and on-line publications. He has been engaged to write and assist on publications by other best-selling writers and successful companies.

Bob's **B**usiness **E**nhancement **S**uccess **T**ools

Leadership, business, and career success series

Running TOO Fast (8th edition 2018)
Legacy of Leadership (3rd edition 2016)
Make ME Feel Special! (6th edition 2016)
Why Didn't I 'THINK' of That? (5th edition 2015)
Speaking for Success! (8th edition 2016)
THINK Beyond the First Sale (3rd edition 2017)
Prepare Yourself to WIN! (3rd edition 2018)

Bob's mini-book success series

The Courage to Lead! (4th edition 2017)
Creative Conflict (3rd edition 2017)
Get to YES! (3rd edition 2017)
THINK Before You Ink! (3rd edition 2017)
Running to Win! (2nd edition 2017)
How to Generate More Sales (4th edition 2017)
Unleash your Business Potential (3rd edition 2017)

Learn to Listen (2nd edition 2017)
Creativity Counts! (3rd edition 2016)
Create Your Future! (3rd edition 2017)

Bob's Pocket Wisdom series
Pocket Wisdom for **Selling Professionals**
Pocket Wisdom for **Speakers**
Pocket Wisdom for **Innovators**
Pocket Wisdom for **Leaders** – Power of One!
Pocket Wisdom for **Business Builders**

Co-authored books created by Bob
Quantum Success – 3 volume series (2006)
In the Company of Leaders (3rd edition 2014)
Foundational Success (2nd edition 2013)

Bob's Idea-rich leaders edge series (2018)
LEAD! *12 idea-rich leadership success strategies*
CREATE! *Idea-rich strategies for enhanced innovation*
TIME! *Idea-rich tips for enhanced performance and productivity*
SERVICE! *Idea-rich strategies for enhanced customer service*
SPEAK! *Idea-rich tips and techniques for great presentations*
CREATIVE CONFLICT *Idea-rich leadership strategies for team success*

Visit: www.SuccessPublications.ca for more information on Bob's publications and other success resources.

Email: bob@ideaman.net or visit:
www.SuccessPublications.ca

"A man who dares to waste one hour of life has not discovered the value of life."
Charles Darwin

What they say about Bob 'Idea Man' Hooey

As I travel across North America, and more recently around the globe, sharing my Ideas At Work! I am fortunate to get feedback and comments from my audiences and colleagues. These comments come from people who have been touched, challenged, or simply enjoyed themselves in one of my sessions.

I'd love to come and share some ideas with your organization and teams.

"I still get comments from people about your presentation. Only a few speakers have left an impression that lasts that long. You hit a spot with the tourism people." **Janet Bell**, Yukon Economic Forums

"Thank you, Bob, it is always a pleasure to see a true professional at work. You have made the name 'Speaker' stand out as a truism - someone who encourages people to examine their lives and adjust. The comments indicated you hit people right where it is important - in their hearts. Each of those in your audience took away a new feeling of personal success and encouragement." **Sherry Knight**, Dimension Eleven Human Resources and Communications

"I am pleased to recommend Bob 'Idea Man' Hooey to any organization looking for a charismatic, confident speaker and seminar leader. I have seen Bob in action on several occasions, and he is ALWAYS on! Bob has the ability to grab his audience's attention and keep it. Quite simply, if Bob is involved - your program or seminar is guaranteed to succeed." **Maurice Laving**, Coordinator Training and Development, London Drugs

"On very short notice Bob cleared his schedule and graciously presented at our meeting when the original Speaker was unable to attend. **Last week Bob set the tone for our two-day leadership meeting and gave us all a motivational lift.** *His compassion and true interest in people was clearly evident, making him very credible. He shared some great stories, has a wealth of experience and knowledge and it was a pleasure listening to him. His down-to-Earth style makes it easier to retain the information presented. He also followed up with additional info and handouts, cementing his message of building bridges, not walls. Fantastic job, Bob, and thanks again!"*
Barbara Afra Beler, MBA, Senior Specialist Commercial Community, Alberta North, **BMO Bank of Montreal**

*"I have been so excited working with Bob Hooey, as he has given inspiration and motivation to our leadership team members. Both at the Brick Warehouse – Alberta and here at Art Van Furniture – Michigan; with his years of experience in working with business executives and his humorous and delightful packaging of his material, he makes **learning with Bob a real joy**. But most importantly, anyone who encounters his material is the better for it."*
Kim Yost, CEO Art Van Furniture, former CEO The Brick

Motivate your teams, your employees, and your leaders to 'productively' grow and 'profitably' succeed!

Protect your conference investment - leverage your training dollars.

Enhance your professional career and sell more products and services.

Equip and motivate your leaders and their teams to grow and succeed, 'even' in tough times!

Leverage your time to enhance your skills, equip your teams, and better serve your clients.

Leverage your leadership and investment of time to leave a significant legacy!

Call today to engage best-selling author, award winning, inspirational leadership keynote speaker, leaders' success coach, and employee development trainer, **Bob 'Idea Man' Hooey** and his innovative, audience based, results-focused, **Ideas At Work!** for your next company, convention, leadership, staff, training, or association event. You'll be glad you did!

Call 1-780-736-0009 to connect with Bob 'Idea Man' Hooey today!

Learn more about Bob at:
www.ideaman.net or
www.BobHooey.training

www.ingramcontent.com/pod-product-compliance
Lightning Source LLC
Chambersburg PA
CBHW030101230526
45471CB00003B/1203